Essential Question
How do we investigate questions about nature?

Norman Borlaug and the Green Revolution

by Jocelyn Cranefield

Chapter 1

An Iowa Boy

Norman Borlaug and his friends were on their way to school when suddenly they were caught in a blizzard. Norman and his friends walked to school in almost all weather, but a neighbor would take them on a horse and sled during very bad storms. However, on this day, the blizzard came up very fast. Norman soon became exhausted from walking in the wind and cold. He decided to lie down in the deep, soft snow, telling the others he could not go on.

His cousin Sina grabbed him, shouting that he had to keep moving. Her behavior made him get back up and continue on his way to school. By not letting him stop and sleep in the blizzard she had saved his life. Years later, Norman said that Sina inspired him by refusing to let him give up that day.

Norman had to walk to school in all kinds of weather.

Norman Borlaug was born on his grandparents' farm in Saude, Iowa, in 1914. He was the eldest of four children. People in this farming community relied on the land to survive, and from a young age Norman had work to do. He helped his family to raise cattle, pigs, and chickens, and to grow oats and corn.

At his one-room country school, the children began each day by singing "The Iowa Corn Song." In the winter, there were 16 students at the school, but in the summer, enrollment dropped to only 10 or 12. The older boys were unable to attend school because they were needed to help harvest the crops instead.

GIVING 105%

During high school, Norman took up baseball and wrestling. He achieved state-wide renown as a competitive wrestler. His wrestling coach always encouraged him to "give 105%." This idea helped him develop a toughness and strength that he would call on later in life.

Norman Borlaug was made a member of the National Wrestling Hall of Fame in 1992.

3

When Norman finished high school, his grandfather encouraged him to keep studying. Norman enrolled at the University of Minnesota, taking odd jobs to help pay his way. This was during the **Great Depression**. Norman was shocked to meet many desperate, hungry people who had lost their jobs, savings, and property.

One day, he heard a scientist at the university talk about microscopic **fungus** spores called rust, which feed on crops and destroy them. The scientist, Dr. Elvin Stakman, described rust as a "shifty enemy." Rust spreads by releasing microscopic spores into the wind, which helps it to travel around the world. Dr. Stakman argued that if science could discover a way to help plants resist rust, world hunger would be reduced. Norman was instantly hooked on the idea. He went on to study with Dr. Stakman.

This wheat stem has rust. Microscopic rust spores are picked up by the wind and carried from plant to plant.

Chapter 2
Borlaug Goes to Mexico

When he finished college in 1942, Norman Borlaug got a job with the DuPont chemical company. But in 1944, his former teacher, Dr. Stakman, encouraged him to join a project working on solving Mexico's food shortage problem.

Mexico needed more food crops for its growing **population**. Borlaug's job was to lead a team of scientists and farmers. They needed to figure out how to grow more wheat on each acre of farmland, increasing the land's **yield**.

YIELD

The only part of wheat used for food is the seed, or grain. Yield is the amount of grain that comes from an area planted with wheat. It is usually expressed as U.S. bushels per acre. One bushel of wheat weighs about 60 pounds. The yield depends on how many heads of wheat there are, the number of seeds, and the size of the seeds. The better the yield, the more people can be fed.

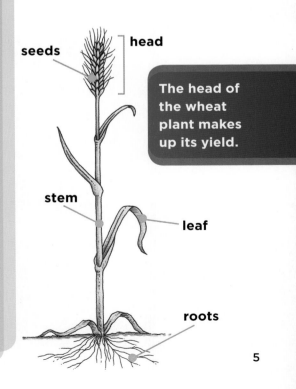

seeds

head

The head of the wheat plant makes up its yield.

stem

leaf

roots

There was another problem: a significant amount of Mexico's wheat crop was being ruined by rust fungus. Borlaug needed to breed wheat that was resistant to rust as quickly as possible. This process would take 10 to 12 years using normal methods. He needed to find a way to speed up the process.

Borlaug started his work at the Yaqui (*YAH-kee*) Valley Experiment Station in Sonora, Mexico. The **research** station was in disrepair, with broken windows and no power, but the conditions in the valley were perfect for growing wheat. The days were warm and sunny, the soil was rich and fertile, and the land was irrigated.

Norman Borlaug had a theory about how to double the rate of breeding wheat by growing it all year round, but his theory meant breaking with tradition. At that time, scientists normally bred plants at a single site. This made it easy to control the growing conditions and compare the results of experiments. They also thought that newly harvested seeds need a rest to store energy before being replanted. So Borlaug's ideas were very innovative.

The Yaqui Valley was a good place to grow wheat in the winter, but in the summer it was too hot. Summer temperatures there reach more than 100 degrees Fahrenheit. If Borlaug could find somewhere else to grow wheat in the summer, he could run his experiments all year long. This might make all the difference in his race to find a solution.

The Yaqui Valley is sometimes called the home of the "green revolution" because of Norman Borlaug's work there.

Chapter 3
A Breakthrough

Norman Borlaug traveled around Mexico, taking note of different climates. He was looking for places where wheat would grow in the summer. Hundreds of miles away, in the cold mountain climate of the south, he found two sites near each other that seemed perfect: Toluca (*toh-LEW-kah*) Valley and Chapingo (*chah-PEEN-goh*).

WHEAT-BREEDING SITES IN MEXICO

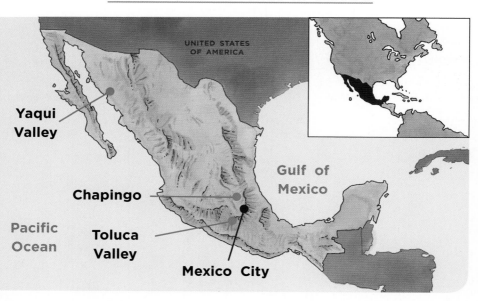

Now Borlaug had two different growing seasons to work with. In the winter, he could grow wheat at the Yaqui Valley site in the north. In the summer, he could grow it at the Toluca Valley and Chapingo sites in the south.

As the years went on, Borlaug and his energetic team shuttled, or moved, many **generations** of plants back and forth between the northern and southern sites. He called this new system "shuttle breeding." With the help of local farmers, Borlaug set about **crossbreeding** different kinds of wheat.

Each time a new generation grew in the Yaqui Valley, he spent hours continuing his observation of the plants. He took notes on their size, how fast they grew, and their resistance to disease. He picked the best plants and crossed them with other successful plants, creating a new generation to grow at the southern sites.

Borlaug's theory had proved correct. By moving plants between sites with different growing seasons, he could do twice as many breeding experiments.

CROSSBREEDING

In crossbreeding, scientists choose plants with features they want to combine. One plant might be fast growing and another might be resistant to disease. Scientists use the pollen from one type of plant to pollinate the other plant. Then scientists combine these plants to create a new variety, called a hybrid. The hybrid has both traits of the parent plants.

Borlaug (third from left) with a group of Mexican farmers in a wheat field.

9

All this testing helped Borlaug and his team to finally develop a **strain** of wheat that could resist disease. While the team was excited about the disappearance of the rust, they found another problem. The new plants produced so much wheat that they often bent over from the weight of their own grain. They were too heavy and tall!

Borlaug started using shorter plants, called dwarfs, in the breeding program. The strong, thick stems of the dwarf wheat plants helped them to stay upright. Even better, they also produced more grain.

By crossing these dwarf plants with the taller wheat, Borlaug's team was able to solve the problem. They developed a new variety of wheat that was disease resistant and short stemmed, and had a higher yield.

Norman Borlaug shows two varieties of wheat.

Norman Borlaug's work in Mexico took more than 15 years, but the project was a huge success. In the end, Borlaug and his team bred more than 40 short, rust-resistant strains of high-yield wheat. When the new strains were grown with fertilizer, they produced two to three times more grain than normal wheat.

The breeding across sites had another benefit, too. The new wheat had been grown in different climates, with different numbers of daylight hours, making it tough and adaptable. Borlaug realized the high-yield semi-dwarf variety could be grown in many places and in varying conditions. This was good news for the rest of the world.

MEXICO'S WHEAT YIELDS BEFORE AND AFTER THE HIGH-YIELD SEMI-DWARF VARIETY

Wheat yield in 1945:
about 250,000 tons

Wheat yield in 1965:
about 2,500,000 tons

After the new wheat strains were planted throughout Mexico, the wheat yield increased from approximately 250,000 tons to approximately 2,500,000 tons. That's a ten-fold increase over a period of 20 years!

Chapter 4
More Wheat for the World

In the 1960s, Norman Borlaug turned his attention to an even bigger problem. India and Pakistan were struggling to produce enough food for their growing populations. Many scientists believed that millions of people could starve if food production was not increased.

Borlaug shipped hundreds of tons of the high-yield wheat seeds to India and Pakistan and worked closely with government officials, explaining how to grow them successfully. He later said that speaking to such powerful leaders took as much courage as stepping onto a wrestling mat.

MEXICO, INDIA, AND PAKISTAN

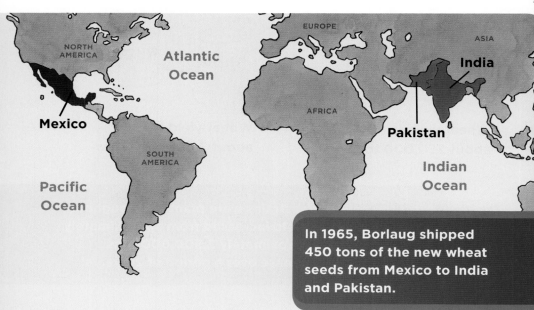

In 1965, Borlaug shipped 450 tons of the new wheat seeds from Mexico to India and Pakistan.

Within a few years, the new types of wheat were growing across many parts of India and Pakistan. Yields increased remarkably. Between 1964 and 2001, Pakistan's wheat production increased from around 4.5 to around 22 million tons. India's rose from around 12 to around 75 million tons!

Mexico's wheat production increased from around 250,000 tons in 1945 to around 1,000,000 tons in 1956, and around 2.5 million tons by 1965—a tenfold increase in 20 years.

It was not just Borlaug's seeds that spread. His ideas started to migrate, too. In a flurry of growth, plant-breeding stations had been set up in India, Pakistan, Canada, the United States, and South America by the late 1960s.

Scientists in these places began working together. They shared test results and sent each other seeds. They changed their behaviors: it was a whole new way of working.

The high-yield wheat grew quickly, but it needed a lot of water and nutrients. Borlaug encouraged farmers to change their traditional practices and to start using **irrigation** and fertilizer. Together, the new plants and these new farming methods were called the "green revolution." Norman Borlaug is known as the father of the "green revolution."

Borlaug taught Indian scientists and farmers about the new wheat.

Early one morning in 1970, Borlaug's wife received an exciting phone call. Her husband had already left for work, so she drove after him to share the news. He was in a wheat field when he found out that he had won the Nobel Peace Prize. Nobody had ever won it for growing plants before!

Norman Borlaug is credited with saving a billion lives. His innovations transformed farming and helped people see that science and technology could lead to improvements in farming. He also helped to build a global community of scientists who could work together on solving problems.

Borlaug's new ideas and dedication helped people all over the world.

Respond to Reading

Summarize

Use important details from *Norman Borlaug and the Green Revolution* to summarize how Norman Borlaug investigated his questions about nature. Your graphic organizer may help you.

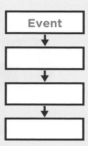

Event

Text Evidence

1. How do you know that *Norman Borlaug and the Green Revolution* is a biography? **GENRE**

2. What was the sequence of events that led Borlaug to work as a plant scientist? Give examples from the text. **SEQUENCE**

3. The suffix *-ic* means "of or like something." For example, adding *-ic* to the noun *metal* forms the adjective *metallic*, meaning "made of or looking like metal." What does *microscopic* on page 4 mean? **GREEK AND LATIN SUFFIXES**

4. Reread Chapter 4. Write about the sequence of events that increased wheat production in India and Pakistan. **WRITE ABOUT READING**

Compare Texts
Read a traditional story that shows the importance of observing nature.

Golden Apples

Each year, Lady Setenaya noticed a remarkable apple growing at the top of her golden apple tree. This apple was very different from the other apples. It took six months to grow—much longer than the rest! It was also larger, rounder, and firmer when it ripened. When fall came, the special apple slowly shrank again.

Patiently, Lady Setenaya watched and waited. When the first frost came, she picked the apple while it was still ripe and juicy.

Over the years, Lady Setenaya tested many different uses for the apple and carefully observed the results.

She found that if people bit into its flesh, they became younger, kinder, and more energetic. If she mashed its core into a cream, it made people's skin soft and radiant. And when she boiled the skin, those who drank the broth became jubilant.

News of the special apple spread. One day, a disease called Cholera disguised itself as an old man and came to her, begging for a taste. Lady Setenaya's powers of observation had grown sharp, and she saw through his sly trickery.

She knew that Cholera would kill more people if he became younger, and so she turned him away. Enraged, he crept back at night and cut down the tree.

Lady Setenaya was greatly distressed; however, she found that she no longer needed the golden apple. Her years of studying nature and observing people had made her a talented natural physician. Very soon, she discovered new **concoctions** to keep her people healthy and happy.

Make Connections

How did Lady Setenaya use observation to investigate questions about nature?
ESSENTIAL QUESTION

How does understanding the seasons help when investigating questions about nature? Use examples from *Norman Borlaug and the Green Revolution* and *Golden Apples* to support your answer. **TEXT TO TEXT**

Glossary

concoctions *(kuhn-KAHK-shuhnz)* mixtures of different ingredients *(page 18)*

crossbreeding *(KRAWS-breed-ing)* combining elements of multiple organisms to make a new variety *(page 9)*

fungus *(FUN-guhs)* a plant-like organism that survives by breaking down other plants and animals *(page 4)*

generations *(jen-uh-RAY-shuhnz)* steps in the ancestry of people, plants, or animals *(page 9)*

Great Depression *(GRAYT di-PRESH-uhn)* a worldwide economic downturn from 1929 to 1939 *(page 4)*

irrigation *(ir-uh-GAY-shuhn)* a system of supplying water to crops *(page 13)*

population *(pop-yuh-LAY-shuhn)* the number of people who live in a country, city, or region *(page 5)*

research *(ri-SURCH)* studying to better understand something *(page 16)*

strain *(strayn)* a variety with ancestors in common *(page 10)*

yield *(yeeld)* the amount produced *(page 5)*

Index

Focus on Science

Purpose To find out about other plants that have been crossbred

Procedure

Step 1 Research real hybrid plants that have been crossbred for specific traits.

Step 2 Pick three of the plants that you want to know more about. Make sure you identify the traits they were bred for and why.

Step 3 For each plant, make a family tree that shows the ancestors and the resulting hybrid. Label each of the ancestors and include their attributes. Make sure you also include the hybrid's attributes.

Step 4 Share your plant family trees with the class. Explain why you chose your plants, and why your hybrid is important.

Conclusion What have you learned about crossbreeding plants? Is crossbreeding always successful? Why or why not? How does crossbreeding help us? If you were going to crossbreed plants, what would you crossbreed? Explain why you chose the plants you did.